the
WATCHTOWER'S
COMING
CRISIS

DANIEL RODRIGUEZ

**CHICK
PUBLICATIONS**
Ontario, Calif 91761

For a complete list of distributors near you,
call (909) 987-0771, or visit
www.chick.com

Copyright ©2009 by Daniel Rodriguez

Published by:
CHICK PUBLICATIONS
PO Box 3500, Ontario, Calif. 91761-1019 USA
Tel: (909) 987-0771
Fax: (909) 941-8128
Web: www.chick.com
Email: postmaster@chick.com
Printed in the United States of America

Cover photo from:
www.everystockphoto.com/photo.php?imageId=1224138

First Printing

ISBN: 978-07589-0674-8

Scripture quotations: King James Version and *The New World
Translation* (Watchtower Bible and Tract Society)

CONTENTS

Endorsements:

Daniel Rodriguez has assembled a telling argument against the absurd claims of Jehovah's Witnesses to be the 144,000 of Revelation 7 and 14. His examination of the history of the Watchtower Society would be of great service to the serious student of the Watchtower movement, or to one who has relatives or friends in the Watchtower. His novel approach to the claim that it is the remnant of the 144,000 who are directing the activity of Jehovah's Witnesses worldwide is thoroughly documented. The format of the book is helpful too, with a summary at the end of each chapter. His approach to Watchtower doctrine leaves even the well-informed Witness unable to use any of his "canned" or rehearsed answers. A very practical and hard-hitting book that will assist the Christian reader to "snatch some from the fire."

Don Nelson, former Bethelite, an official who worked at Watchtower headquarters. Also in charge of Watchtower missions in Brazil for several years.

This book is amazing! It explains so simply how to approach the Jehovah's Witnesses at our front door with compassion and love. The book gave us more confidence to witness the truth… and to deprogram the lies in the minds of the JW's.

Eric and Babette Peterson,
Radio and Deliverance Ministries

Daniel Rodriguez successfully unravels the Watchtower's deceitful attempts to adjust the historical timeline and cover up the fact that the original 144,000 Jehovah's Witnesses are dying off. I highly recommend this revelation of the inner machinations of the Watchtower Society.

Fernando Borrego, student of cults and mind control

I have debated many Jehovah's Witnesses, and have left sometimes seriously defeated as I did not know proper procedures in dealing with them. Daniel's approach puts an entirely new weapon in the hands of those who read this book. His loving and kind approach demonstrates the love of Christ; yet cuts to the cancer of false doctrine like a surgeon's scalpel, and applies a healing balm at the same time. I recommend it very highly!

Chuck Thomas, missionary to Israel

…a formidable "weapon" for setting members of the Jehovah's Witness cult free… Few people share Daniel Rodriguez's knowledge of the devious ways of the Watchtower Society and fewer still have assembled that knowledge in a useful format for those who have a passion to see Jesus set free those held captive in this strange and heavily religious cult.

Dr. Tom Wymore, Foursquare Church Leader in Colorado

The information in this book is remarkably on target! Had I known it, I would have never become a part of this "organization." I would have been spared much pain…

Sally Korell, ex-Jehovah's Witness

Preface

Chances are you have never met a real "Jehovah's Witness." While those at your door may claim to be one, their own publications plainly teach otherwise.

So who are the *real* Jehovah's Witnesses?

The Watchtower Society teaches that anyone who claims to be one of Jehovah's Witnesses must one of the 144,000, the *only* ones who go to heaven. Membership in this group began with the early apostles. Over the centuries others were added but the number was completed in 1935, so any real Jehovah's Witness would be very old. Once the last of these 144,000 die, the Jehovah's Witnesses will no longer have leadership, and the organization must cease to exist. Time is running out!

These 144,000 are the only ones who hear from God and are responsible for all Watchtower teaching and leadership.

Because these people have been dying off, the Watchtower has been facing a credibility crisis. So they have been quietly manipulating the death figures to keep the organization alive.

In 2007, the organization tried to wiggle out of the 1935 closing date for the 144,000. But this only adds further opportunity for you to show the "JW" who comes to your door that he cannot trust this organization with his precious eternal life.

The representative at your door believes he will remain on "Paradise Earth" after the coming Armageddon, since only the original 144,000 have any hope of going to heaven. (They are also the only ones allowed to *take communion*.)

He does not believe he can understand Bible truths without the *Watchtower*. He is dependent on a publication that, one day soon, will be left without writers to reveal God's truths. Who are those writers? Those who remain of the original 144,000. And they are dying!

Oddly enough, their founder, Charles Taze Russell, *never taught* the doctrine of the 144,000. In this book, you will learn the true history of this false Watchtower doctrine. You will be surprised to discover that it is not just a Bible issue. It is also a historical issue and a numbers game.

The dying off of the original 144,000 threatens to leave the Watchtower Society with a terrible leadership void. This is planting seeds of doubt in the minds of its followers which undermine the Watchtower's authority. Their leaders know this cornerstone doctrine must remain alive if the Watchtower is to continue existing as the spiritual leader for its followers. Time is the enemy of this teaching and they know it.

The clock is ticking.

THE FAITHFUL AND DISCREET SLAVE: A BRIEF HISTORY

> Who really is the *faithful and discreet slave*
> whom his master appointed over his domestics,
> to give them their food at the proper time?
> Happy is that slave if his master on arriving
> finds him doing so.[1]

This is the foundation scripture the Watchtower cites as its authority. It is found in Matthew 24 of the Jehovah's Witness Bible, where Jesus spoke of the signs of the end. Modern literature teaches that this "*slave*" is the Watchtower organization. According to them, this *faithful and discreet slave* is, in these "last days," carrying Jehovah's message of escape from the destruction of Armageddon.

The Watchtower claims to be the modern-day *ark of salvation*. Like Noah after the flood, the Witnesses believe they will live in a New World Society after Armageddon.

> The flood was a real physical catastrophe to the
> old ungodly world. The Battle of Armageddon

1 Matthew 24:45-46, *New World Translation*, 1984 edition (Italics added)

> will be likewise a physical catastrophe to this present evil world, and not something just spiritual. The ark of salvation that we enter is not a literal ark but is God's organization ...[2]

But that was not always so. In the early days they were known as *Bible Students*. But...

> At the Columbus, Ohio, convention in 1931, fitting application was made of Isaiah 43:10-12. *The Bible Students adopted the distinctive name Jehovah's Witnesses.*[3]

> ...notably down to the year 1931 when the *anointed remnant* embraced the Scripturally backed designation "*Jehovah's Witnesses.*"[4]

The *anointed remnant* are those of the original 144,000 Jehovah's Witnesses who remain alive. Therefore, the name *Jehovah's Witnesses* only applies to them.

> Thus no real gathering and organizing of these marked ones, the "other sheep," was encouraged, even in the year 1931, *when the remnant of the 144,000 spiritual Israelites embraced the name Jehovah's witnesses.*[5]

Four years after the "remnant" of the 144,000 adopted the name Jehovah's Witnesses in 1931, they were further identified as the *faithful and discreet slave*. Those who came to the Watchtower *after* 1935 became known as the *other*

---

2 *The Watchtower*, June 1, 1950, p. 176
3 *The Watchtower*, January 15, 2001, p. 19
4 *Paradise Restored To Mankind —By Theocracy!*, 1972, p. 105 (Italics added)
5 *The Watchtower*, February 15, 1966, p. 119 (Italics added)

sheep, **not** Jehovah's Witnesses. This is why those at your door *are not* truly Jehovah's Witnesses if they came to the Watchtower *after* 1935. The following quote further clarifies this distinction between the two classes:

> After all, Revelation 12:17 warns us that Satan is 'waging war' with the anointed remnant. Because of *their close association with the anointed*, the "*other sheep*" are likewise targets of Satan's wrath.[6]

Other references call them the *great crowd* or the *great multitude*. While the 144,000 will enjoy life in heaven, the *other sheep* will remain on *paradise earth*. As *companions*, they assist the remnant of the 144,000 by taking the message of the Watchtower door-to-door. They do not expect to ever go to heaven.

> At the Washington, D.C., convention in 1935, it was thrilling to learn that the *great multitude*, or *great crowd*, of Revelation chapter 7 is *a class with an earthly hope*.[7]

Main Proselytizing Tool

At this writing, the main publication used to proselytize individuals is "What Does The Bible Really Teach?" It has some basic Watchtower theology, but is "watered down" so as not to frighten away prospective converts by their more radical Bible interpretations. This publication uses biblical references only as a ploy to convert people. When they come

---

6 *The Watchtower*, August 15, 2001, p. 25 (Italics added)
7 *The Watchtower*, January 15, 2001, p. 19 (Italics added)

to trust this publication, they are taken deeper into Watchtower interpretation of Scripture. The topic of the *faithful and discreet slave* is not discussed in this publication. That is taught after the individual has blindly submitted to basic Watchtower teaching.

Summary:

• The Watchtower Society has identified itself as the *faithful and discrete slave* of Matthew 24:45. This is their foundation scripture.

• In 1931, the early "Bible Students" came to be called "Jehovah's Witnesses" of Isaiah 43:10-12.

• In 1935, it was decided that the existing "Jehovah's Witnesses" were an "anointed remnant" of the 144,000. Membership was closed and all who joined after that belonged to the great crowd of Rev. 7:9.

• The name Jehovah's Witnesses only applies to the 144,000. Those who came to the organization after 1935 are called *companions, great crowd, other sheep, great multitude* or *earthly class.*

• The "remnant" are those who remain alive of the original 144,000 identified as the *faithful and discreet slave* class in 1935.

• Only the 144,000 are "born again," can receive communion, and expect to go to heaven. All others only have an earthly hope, not heavenly. They will inhabit *paradise earth* after Armageddon.

Who Was The Faithful and Discreet Slave?

Most of today's *companions* are unaware that the identity of the *faithful and discreet slave* has changed over the years. Charles T. Russell founded what is now known as the Watchtower Bible and Tract Society in the 1870s. He, alone, was known to his "Bible students" as the *faithful and discreet slave* or *faithful and wise servant* of Matthew 24:45.

When he died in 1916, there was a controversy over who would pick up the mantle. Watchtower literature from that era indicates a shift away from a person (Russell) as the "slave" to the Watchtower organization itself. An early Watchtower publication referred to:

> "...that wise and faithful servant of the Lord
> —CHARLES TAZE RUSSELL."[8]

> Thousands of the readers of Pastor Russell's writings believe that he filled the office of that faithful and wise servant, and that his great work was giving to the household of faith meat in due season. *His modesty and humility pre-*

8 *The Finished Mystery*, 1917, p. 5

> *cluded him from openly claiming this title*, but
> *he admitted as much in private conversation.*[9]

After Russell's death, the Watchtower attempted to distance itself from him being that *faithful and wise servant*. In 1982, *Watchtower* magazine taught:

> This 'faithful and discreet slave' is comprised of
> faithful Christians, wholly dedicated to Jehovah
> through Christ and begotten by God's spirit.
> They are earnest Bible students who, since the
> mid-1870s, have come out strongly in defend-
> ing the Bible as God's Word by means of books,
> booklets, magazines and tracts, newspaper
> articles and public lectures. In 1886, they pub-
> lished Volume I of Studies in the Scriptures.[10]

This statement is a lie. Beginning in 1886, Russell published a series of six books titled, *Studies In The Scriptures*. Volume I was titled, *The Divine Plan of the Ages*, written by "Pastor Russell" in 1886. This statement attempts to shift the attention away from Russell by saying the *faithful and discreet slave* was made up of "faithful Christians" who would become known in the 1930s as the 144,000. Today, they claim that the *faithful and discreet slave* (the Watchtower Society) published *The Divine Plan of the Ages*.

After Russell died, a seventh volume of his *Studies in the Scriptures* was released and titled, *The Finished Mystery*. This book hailed Russell as that *wise and faithful servant*.

In the latter half of 1917 the faithful forefront

---

9 *The Divine Plan of the Ages*, 1886, p. 7, 1927 edition (Italics added)
10 *The Watchtower*, March 15, 1982, p. 21 (Italics added)

preachers of the "discreet slave" class energetically took up distribution of *The Finished Mystery*.[11]

Today those remaining of this anointed remnant are known worldwide as Jehovah's Witnesses. They were also his witnesses back there in 1918.

...the anointed remnant were publishing and circulating that commentary on the entire book of Revelation, *The Finished Mystery*, besides Bibles and six volumes of *Studies in the Scriptures* that discussed the entire Bible.[12]

Two Problems:

1. How could the Watchtower say the *anointed remnant* "were his [Jehovah's] witnesses" in 1918 when the teaching did not exist until 1935? This appears to be an attempt to blend the name back into the history of the movement.

2. How could the Watchtower say the "*discreet slave class* energetically took up distribution of *The Finished Mystery* when this *same book* declared Charles T. Russell to be the *faithful and wise servant* of the Lord?

Remember:

The *slave class* teaching did not exist until 1935. Russell never taught the doctrine of the 144,000 because he and his followers believed him alone to be the *faithful and wise*

---

11 *The Watchtower*, April 1, 1955, p. 206
12 *Then Is Finished The Mystery Of God*, 1969, p. 264 (Italics added, complete title)

servant or *faithful and discreet slave.* This confirms there was no belief in the 144,000 during the time of Russell.

Even after his death, some still believed that Russell was that *faithful and wise servant* because *The Finished Mystery* declared him to be so. The Watchtower attempted to distance itself from those people by stating they were involved in creature worship:

> With the passing of time, however, the idea adopted by many was that C. T. Russell himself was the "faithful and wise servant." *This led some into the snare of creature worship.* They felt that all the truth God saw fit to reveal to his people had been presented through Brother Russell, that nothing more could be brought forth.[13]

This accusation was designed to squelch the previous teaching that C. T. Russell himself was the *faithful and wise servant.* Such an admission would have forced them to also admit that there was no 144,000 during Russell's time. So they tried to blame the "People's Pulpit Association" for calling Russell the "faithful and discreet slave" when it really should have been the Watchtower Society:

> However, the sense of appreciation and indebtedness toward Russell moved many of his associates to view him as the fulfillment of the "faithful and discreet slave." This view was prominently featured in the book published in July of 1917 by *People's Pulpit Association*

---

13 *1975 Yearbook of Jehovah's Witnesses*, 1974, p. 88

of Brooklyn, New York. This book was called
'The Finished Mystery'...[14]

Who was the "People's Pulpit Association?":

Such a corporation came into legal existence
February 23, 1909. Thirty years later, in 1939,
the name was changed to its present one, Watch-
tower Bible and Tract Society, Inc.[15]

The Watchtower realized that *The Finished Mystery* promoted Russell as that *faithful and wise servant*, contradicting
the later teaching that it was the 144,000 "servant class."
In the preface of *The Finished Mystery*, not one word stated
the *faithful and wise servant* was any 144,000; only Russell.[16]

At the end of this preface is the name of the organization
that endorsed *The Finished Mystery* —Watchtower BIBLE
AND TRACT SOCIETY; the *same* organization that said
Russell was that *faithful and wise servant*. So while they were
accusing others of creature worship, they were distributing
The Finished Mystery, which said that Russell was the *faithful
and wise servant*. They were actually blaming themselves.

To further cover their tracks, in 1973 the Watchtower
quoted an 1881 Zion's Watch Tower article written by Russell, where the whole body "individually and collectively"
was giving meat in due season; and then the Watchtower
lied by stating that Russell never claimed to be that faithful
and wise servant:

---

14 *God's Kingdom Of A Thousand Years Has Approached*, 1973, pp. 346-347
(Italics added)
15 *Qualified To Be Ministers*, 1955, p. 309 (Italics added)
16 *The Finished Mystery*, 1917 preface, p. 5

> From this it is clearly seen that the editor and
> publisher of Zion's Watch Tower disavowed
> any claim to being, individually in his person,
> that "faithful and wise servant." *He never did
> claim to be such.*[17]

Keep in mind what the Watchtower said before:

> Thousands of the readers of Pastor Russell's
> writings believe that he filled the office of
> "that faithful and wise servant," and that his
> great work was giving to the household of
> faith meat in due season. His modesty and
> humility precluded him from openly claiming
> this title, but he admitted as much in private
> conversation.[18]

The Watchtower's own historical literature clearly states
that Russell was the *faithful and discreet slave,* not the 144,000
anointed Jehovah's Witnesses.

More Evidence

Another issue of The Watchtower teaches:

> John, in another vision, sees the sealing of the
> final ones of the 144,000 (Revelation 7:1-8).
> Evidently, *the gathering of these was virtually
> complete by 1935.*[19]

Why are these historical facts so important? From time to

---

17 *God's Kingdom of a Thousand Years Has Approached,* 1973, p. 346 (Italics
added)
18 *The Divine Plan of the Ages,* C.T. Russell Biography, 1886, p. 7, 1927
edition (Italics added)
19 *The Watchtower,* January 1, 1988, p. 11 (Italics added)

time, the Watchtower has been forced to *adjust* the teachings and "facts" of their history.

> Things published were not perfect in the days of Charles Taze Russell, first president of the Watch Tower Bible and Tract Society; nor were they perfect in the days of J. F. Rutherford, the succeeding president. The increasing light on God's Word as well as *the facts of history have repeatedly required that adjustments of one kind or another be made down to the very present time.*[20]

These "adjustments" cast further doubt on the Watchtower's claim to speak for God. If it was truly inspired, such adjustments would not be necessary. Watchtower records not only confirm that Russell was seen as that *faithful and wise servant*, but that they "adjusted" this history. *This allowed them to claim that the 144,000 had always existed as that servant.*

The *Bible Students* were in trouble. From whom would they receive spiritual direction if Russell was dead? Without this *faithful and wise servant*, there would be no direction or communication from Jehovah God. It was *crucial* that this "organism" remain alive and breathing or the Watchtower Society would cease to exist. Thus the invention of the *faithful and wise servant* "class," the 144,000. But by stating that this "class" was full in 1935, they created another dilemma. We shall now see how they maneuver to get out of this one.

---

20 *The Watchtower*, March 1, 1979 pp. 23 -24 (Italics added)

Summary

• Early Watchtower history documents Charles Taze Russell as the *faithful and wise servant.*

• Russell wrote six books titled, *Studies In The Scriptures.* However, the Watchtower now credits the early Bible Students with writing *The Divine Plan of the Ages,* which was Volume I of that series.

• With Russell's death, there was no longer a teacher who spoke for God. So they shifted attention away from Russell being the *faithful and wise servant* by stating the early Bible Students wrote Volume I.

• The Watchtower said the *faithful and discreet slave* class published and distributed *The Finished Mystery,* Volume VII. But Charles Taze Russell authored all seven volumes of the *Studies In The Scriptures.*

• *The Finished Mystery* proclaimed Russell as that *wise and faithful servant.* How could any *faithful and discreet slave class* publish and distribute *The Finished Mystery* since that book said Russell was that *servant?*

• The Watchtower accused those who believed Russell was that *servant* of "creature worship."

• The Watchtower blamed the People's Pulpit Organization for publishing *The Finished Mystery,* but that was the early name of the Watchtower Bible and Tract Society. So they were essentially blaming themselves.

• The Watchtower said Russell never claimed to be that wise and faithful servant but Russell himself admitted as much in private conversations.

3
Gathering The Watchtower's 144,000

With Russell dead, there was no one to fulfill the Watchtower's interpretation of Matthew 24:45. Without this *faithful and wise servant*, there was no one to lead the *companions*. The Watchtower needed to replace Russell to continue. In 1935, it was settled: the new *faithful and wise servant* would not be an individual, it would be the 144,000. It was also decided that this would be taught as if it had always existed.

So how and when were the 144,000 as the *faithful and wise servant* gathered?:

> Jehovah has established a limited number, 144,000, to make up the little flock, and he has been gathering it since Pentecost 33 C.E. Logically, the calling of the little flock would draw to a close when the number was nearing completion, *and the evidence is that the general gathering of these specially blessed ones ended in 1935.*[21]

By providing the ransom sacrifice of Jesus

---

21 *The Watchtower*, February 15, 1995, p. 19 (Italics added)

> Christ, God began gathering the 144,000 almost 2,000 years ago, and *indications are that this group is now complete.*[22]

> God began gathering the 144,000 two thousand years ago during the age of the apostles since Pentecost 33 C.E.[23]

How could it take until 1935 to reach only 144,000 believers? According to the Watchtower, many lost their place as a "great apostasy" overtook the early church, causing millions to fall away and lose their heavenly calling.

> Even so, following the great apostasy after the death of the apostles...[24]

The Watchtower does not claim to know how "many anointed were gathered in the first century," or "during the dark centuries of Christendom's great apostasy." Nor do they know which number they were at when they stopped counting so they could pick up at the next number in counting the 144,000. Nor do they know how the number was finally reached in 1935.

> In the 1930's the number of 'those called and chosen and faithful,' the 144,000, appeared to be filled. *We do not know how many of the anointed were gathered* in the first century and from among the "weeds" during the dark centuries of Christendom's great apostasy.[25]

---

22 *The Watchtower*, October 1, 2000, p. 6 (Italics added)
23 C.E.: Common Era
24 *The Watchtower*, July 1, 1998, p. 12
25 *The Watchtower*, February 1, 1999, p. 17 (Italics added)

So, of all the millions of people in the last 2,000 years, only a mere 144,000 were found faithful. In 1931, they were identified as Jehovah's Witnesses. By 1935, the number of 144,000 as the *faithful and discreet slave* was fulfilled.

Summary:

• Although the Watchtower used to promoted Russell as the *faithful and discreet slave*, they now teach that the gathering of the 144,000 started in 33 A.D.

• After the death of the Apostles, there was a great apostasy of the church.

• Although the Watchtower does not know how many anointed were gathered in the first century and during the "great apostasy," they still somehow knew that the 144,000 was fulfilled in 1935.

144,000: The Aging Class

Since membership in the 144,000 "anointed remnant" was closed in 1935, members of this "remnant" would have to be very old, and only a handful could possibly remain alive today.

Fortunately we have a way to check the numbers. The Watchtower Society tracks the number of those who partake of the communion elements at the annual Memorial service. Since receiving the communion elements is restricted to the remnant class of the 144,000, this enables them to determine how many of the remnant remain alive.

Mysteriously, since 1970 the remnant figure has remained in the 8,000-plus range. The numbers should have dropped due to death. But they somehow stopped going down. (See Figure 1.) The Watchtower has yet to explain why.

The December 15, 1988, *Watchtower* reported that:

> In 1935 attendance worldwide at the Memorial observance of Jesus' death was 32,795. Of these attendees, 27,006 partook of the emblems as being the remaining ones on earth of the 144,000, whose hope is heavenly.[26]

However, in the August 15, 1996 *Watchtower* those numbers were "adjusted":

> For example, at the Memorial celebration in 1935, attended by 63,146, those partaking of the emblems in evidence of their profession to be anointed numbered 52,465.[27]

Comparing the 1988 and 1996 figures, an additional 25,459 were added with no explanation. These "adjustments" would continue, as you will soon see.

The Watchtower officially recognized that the remnant class was advancing in years:

> There is every reason to believe that the number of anointed ones will continue to decline as advanced age and unforeseen occurrences end their earthly lives.[28]

In 1958, 15,037 of the anointed remnant who came to the organization before 1935 were said to be still alive.[29]

---

26 *The Watchtower*, December 15, 1988, p. 12
27 *The Watchtower*, August 15, 1996, p. 31
28 Ibid.
29 *The Watchtower*, January 1, 1958, p. 30

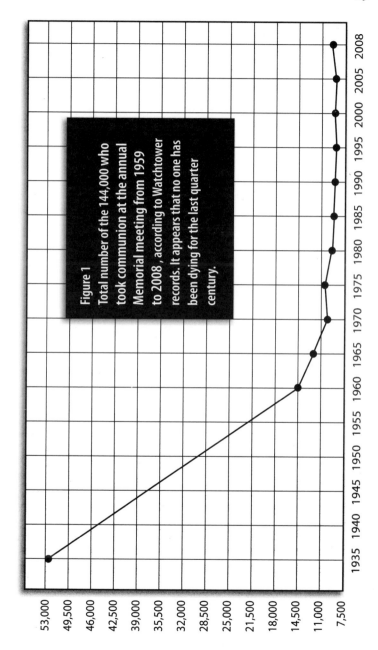

Figure 1

Total number of the 144,000 who took communion at the annual Memorial meeting from 1959 to 2008 , according to Watchtower records. It appears that no one has been dying for the last quarter century.

If the December 15, 1988 *Watchtower* is correct that there were 27,006 alive in 1935, then only 11,969 Jehovah's Witnesses of the remnant died between 1935 and 1958. But if the August 15, 1996 *Watchtower* is correct, then 37,428 Jehovah's Witnesses of the remnant died between 1935 and 1958. The difference has never been explained.

In 1970, President Franz was asked, Who are the newly associated ones who were partaking of the memorial emblems? His only out was to label them as replacements for those who may have fallen away.[30] At that time, he declared: "No, no more additions!"

> At a Gilead graduation in 1970, Frederick Franz, then vice-president of the Watch Tower Society, told the students of the possibility that they, who were all of the other sheep with earthly hopes, might baptize someone who might claim to be of the anointed remnant. Could this happen?
>
> "No, no more additions!" he said. "That call ended way back there in 1931–35! *There are no more additions*. Who, then, are the few newly associated ones who are partaking of the Memorial emblems? If they are of the remnant, they are replacements! *They are not additions to the ranks of the anointed, but replacements for those who may have fallen away.*[31]

---

30 *The Watchtower*, February 1, 1999, p. 19
31 Ibid. (Italics added)

Franz recognized that these "additions" destroyed the foundational teaching that the 144,000 was a closed number, and compromised the 144,000 figure. *But the Watchtower is still adding!*

This same issue was addressed in 1961, although no "replacements" were recorded until years later.

> However, it is likely from among such [*great crowd*] that individuals are called to fill any vacancy in the 144,000 caused by unfaithfulness and rejection. So the date of one's dedicating oneself would have some bearing on the likelihood of one's being of the remnant, although it would not be conclusive.[32]

The Watchtower continued to teach that the 144,000 was completed in 1935. Could any of these people be rejected and replaced? We shall discuss that in the next section.

Summary:

• Membership in the 144,000 was closed in 1935. Any of that group still alive must be very old.

• In 1988, **27,006** of the anointed remnant took part in the Memorial in 1935. But in 1996, they raised that number to **52,465** —a difference of **25,459**.

• From 1970 to 2008, "replacements" were added to the 144,000 to replace Witnesses who had fallen away or given their "inheritance" to someone else.

• Watchtower Vice President Fred Franz said of this,

---

32 *The Watchtower*, March 15, 1961, p. 167

"No, no more additions!" He declared that the jump in the remnant figures represented *replacements*.

• A replacement is a one-for-one exchange without changing the total; but the number is growing.

"Replacing" The 144,000

Is it possible for any of the "anointed" to fall away, and need to be replaced?

> It is reasonable to conclude, therefore, that by that time [1935] the full number of 144,000 would have been nearly completed. Of course, any individuals proving unfaithful would need to be replaced. But, understandably, these would be comparatively few.[33]

But who could replace them?

> Accordingly, should one of these yet on earth prove unfaithful, his position would have to be filled by a replacement. (1 Cor. 9:27; Rev. 3:11) By whom? It could be by a newly baptized person, or it could be by one of the 'great crowd' who has been proving himself a keeper of integrity under test up to that point of time. We cannot limit Jehovah God or Christ Jesus in such selection.[34]

Although this comment was made in 1970, the *Watchtower* also said in 1982:

> They [*great crowd*] *would retain their natural*

---

33 *The Watchtower*, February 1, 1982, p. 28 (Italics added)
34 *The Watchtower*, June 15, 1970, p. 383

hope of living on earth, not being "born again"
with heavenly life in view.[35]

There are only two classes of individuals in the organization: the 144,000 "Jehovah's Witnesses" and their *great crowd companions*. These have entirely different hopes, spiritual positions, and destinies. There does not appear to be any provision for crossover from one to the other. In fact, anyone who presumes to move from the *great crowd* to the 144,000 comes under a cloud of suspicion and even severe judgment.

In 1989 the *Watchtower* restated the issue:

> The 'great crowd' of true Christians today do not need to be born again, since their hope of everlasting life is earthly, not heavenly."[36]

Even in 1954, the distinction between the two was stated:

> Today a 'great crowd' of these 'other sheep' has been gathered into Jehovah's New World society: 'A great crowd, which no man was able to number, out of all nations and tribes and peoples and tongues.' This 'great crowd' of people are not 'born again,' *nor do they need to be 'born again,' because they gain everlasting life on the earth.*[37]

If no provision is made for a crossover from *great crowd* to the "anointed remnant," where does that leave those who were added over the years? Could they not be considered imposters?

---

35 *The Watchtower*, February 15, 1982, p. 30 (Italics added)

36 *The Watchtower*, April 1, 1988, p. 18 (Italics added)

37 *The Watchtower*, November 15, 1954, p. 682 (Italics added)

In fact, the Watchtower views with suspicion anyone who presumes to make that crossover, as was stated in 1982:

> Any who in comparatively recent times dedicated themselves and were baptized and who consider themselves to be "born again" would do well to reflect seriously on the following questions: What reasons have you for feeling that Jehovah God has planted this hope in you? *Could it be that your emotional feeling is a holdover from the mistaken belief you previously held while in Babylon the Great that heaven is the destiny of all good people? Or could it be that you feel this way because you had great inward disturbances, that you at first fought against the idea but it gradually won out? But did it win out because you wanted it that way, perhaps even unconsciously? Such struggles do not of themselves prove that you were 'born again.'*[38]

This *Watchtower* article appears to strongly discourage anyone from professing to be of the anointed class. Mention was made again in 1985 of those who professed to be of the anointed remnant. Bear in mind that no more additions would be recorded for another four years:

> With the foregoing in mind, we say to all those who have recently become associated with Jehovah's people and who may have made some claim to being one of the anointed class: *Examine carefully your relationship with Jehovah.*

---

38 *The Watchtower*, February 1, 1982, p. 28 (Italics added)

> *Ask yourself, Is the heavenly hope that I profess to have somehow a holdover from a previously held church teaching that all church members go to heaven? Is my hope in any way connected with some selfish desire or emotional feelings?* Paul said: "It is impossible for God to lie." (Hebrews 6:18) Nor can the holy spirit of adoption lie. Therefore, anyone genuinely begotten by God's spirit is not continually disturbed with doubts but is able to testify in all good conscience that he is one of God's sons.[39]

These two *Watchtower* statements are meant to discourage those who, after 1935, claim to be of the anointed class. They *do not* encourage them to pursue a heavenly calling. Of those who professed to be of the anointed class, another *Watchtower* article says:

> All who make this claim, however, would do well to ask themselves if their conviction is a holdover from the Babylonish teaching that all good persons go to heaven; or whether it could be due to a misconception, emotionalism, or even a misguided seeking for prominence.[40]

Any member of the *companion* class is consistently discouraged from believing he might replace one of the fallen anointed. He must negatively question any feelings or motives he might have in desiring to be one of the anointed:

> So they [the great crowd] do not partake of

---

39 *The Watchtower*, February 15, 1985, p. 21 (Italics added)
40 *The Watchtower*, June 15, 1970, p. 383-384

the Memorial emblems, for they are not com-
manded by Jesus Christ the Right Shepherd
to do so. They do not want to misrepresent
themselves and eat and drink judgment against
themselves because of sinning against what the
body and blood of the Lord signify. They let
those who are worthy eat and drink.[41]

In other words, the Memorial meal is only for those who
are "worthy" — the remnant of the 144,000 — those who
came to the organization before 1935, not after.

If these older *great crowd* members believe the Watchtower organization is of Jehovah God, and have dedicated
their life in the service of Jehovah through "His organization," would it be worth it, after all these years of service, to
risk judgment by partaking of the emblems and declaring
themselves to be one of the anointed as a replacement? The
Watchtower doesn't think so:

As to the possibility of being a 'born again'
replacement at this late hour, understandably
only a very few of these remaining anointed
ones are likely to forfeit their heavenly calling
by becoming unfaithful.[42]

They are simply doctoring the numbers to forestall the
crisis. The Watchtower knows this is flawed teaching and is
stalling for time. The day will come when they will have to
admit that the original anointed remnant are all gone. Then
there will be no leadership, guidance or spiritual direction.

---

41 *The Watchtower*, February 15, 1952, p. 112 (Italics added)
42 *The Watchtower*, February 15, 1982 pp. 30-31

Summary:

• The Watchtower is playing a numbers game. They have published two contradictory numbers for the "anointed remnant" who were alive in 1935. Their annual yearbook numbers have been doctored to keep from running out of the 144,000.

• Leaders attempted to explain the added numbers as "replacements" for the few members who became "unfaithful." Yet strong suspicion is cast on anyone who claims to be a replacement and severe judgment is pronounced on anyone who is wrong.

• Since members of the *great crowd* need not be "born again," and cannot take communion, they lack the basic qualification to become a member of the 144,000 as a replacement.

• Consequently, there is little hope of them (or anyone) replacing a member of the 144,000.

• "Replacements" would always have the fear of being wrong and the looming threat of judgment.

• "Replacements" are an obvious attempt to defuse the looming crisis brought on by their declaration that the 144,000 was closed in 1935.

144,000: A Sealed Number

The Watchtower Society has an even greater problem. The 144,000 *faithful and discrete slave class* they created in no way resembles the 144,000 described in the Bible.

They say the gathering of the 144,000 began in A.D. 33. But how could any gathering have taken place since the "tribulation" has not even started? In Revelation 7:14, the *great crowd* and 144,000 come out of the great tribulation. And they both appear together before the throne[43] in God's temple[44] in heaven.[45] All of this occurs after the great tribulation.

Even the Watchtower agrees with the Bible that the great tribulation has not yet started.

> Rather, he [Jesus] was pointing to the start of the great tribulation to befall the world system in the future, climaxing his promised "presence." (Matthew 24:3) *That tribulation is still ahead of us.*[46]

Furthermore, the Bible says these 144,000 will be *sealed* out of the "great tribulation." If the Watchtower's interpretation were true, is it possible that there are individual replacements for the 144,000? The Bible says, "No." This is a sealed number. The New World Translation states:

> And I heard the number of those who were sealed, a hundred and forty-four thousand, sealed out of every tribe of the sons of Israel.[47]

Question:

What were they sealed with?

> And I saw, and, look! the Lamb standing upon the Mount Zion, and with him a hundred and

---

43 See Revelation 7:9; 14:3
44 See Revelation 7:15
45 See Revelation 11:19; 14:17
46 *The Watchtower*, February 15, 1994, p. 19 (Italics added)
47 Revelation 7:4, *New World Translation*, 1984 edition

> forty-four thousand *having his name and the name of his Father written on their foreheads.*[48]

Strong's Concordance says the Greek word *sealed*:

> …is to stamp (with a signet or private mark) for security or preservation. It is used to indicate security and permanency. With respect to Revelation 7:3-5, ownership and security, together with destination.[49]

The Jehovah's Witnesses and their *companions* know the name of the Lamb's Father is JEHOVAH. It is His name that will be permanently secured on the foreheads of each of the 144,000. God is saying, "These are mine!" This fact alone rules out the possibility of replacements.

In John 17, Jesus prayed to His Father that those whom God had given Him would be kept through His own Name.[50] Will Jehovah answer Jesus' prayer, then allow members of His 144,000 to fall away?

No.

1 Peter 1:5 says those who are begotten of God "… *are kept by the power of God through faith* unto salvation ready to be revealed in the last time."[51] This argues against the possibility that a member of the 144,000 could become "unsealed" and fall away.

In Revelation 7, John saw four angels standing on the four corners of the earth ready to "bring hurt to the earth."

---

48 Revelation 14:1 *New World Translation*, 1984 edition (Italics added)
49 *Strong's Exhaustive Concordance*, 2001
50 See John 17:11-12
51 KJV (Italics added)

In verse two, another angel cries out with a loud voice to these four angels and says:

> Hurt not the earth, neither the sea, nor the trees, till we have sealed... an hundred and forty and four thousand of all the tribes of the children of Israel.[52]

The angel in Revelation 7:3 instructed the four angels not to bring hurt to the earth until the 144,000 were sealed.

If they were fulfilled and sealed in 1935, why have the angels not been loosed to bring hurt to the earth?

Let's look more carefully at the Biblical description.

The Bible's 144,000

Revelation 7:5-8 lists the twelve tribes that each of the 12,000 male virgins will come from. (12,000 from each of the 12 tribes equals 144,000.) This leads us to another problem. The Watchtower agrees that the number 144,000 is a literal number, which is apparent from the context that tells of a *great crowd*, which no man was able to number."— Revelation 7:3, 4, 9; 14:1, 3; 20:4, 6.[53]

However, they then claim the twelve tribes are figurative:

> No, for further judging is to be carried out by Christ and his under priests after that tribulation. It is the judging of the *figurative* "twelve tribes of Israel," peoples other than the royal priesthood.[54]

---

52 Revelation 7:3-4 KJV
53 *The Watchtower*, February 1, 1982,, p. 22
54 *The Watchtower*, March 1, 1987,, p. 29 (Italics added)

In the Greek text of Revelation 7, the word *phule*, translated "tribe" is used. It is also translated, race, or clan: a company of people united by kinship or habitation, a clan, or tribe, of peoples of the earth.[55]

These are literal tribes (*phule*). Whenever the children of Israel are mentioned in scripture, they are referred to by tribe — a literal people — Jews. The Watchtower has no evidence to support their claim that these tribes are figurative.

Other Problems

The Biblical 144,000 are all males and have never had sexual relations:

> These are they which were not defiled with women; for they are virgins.[56]

This text is speaking of literal males who are literal virgins.

In the Watchtower's own words, the gathering of the 144,000 has not even started. Once they start to gather, they will be sealed out of each tribe of the children of Israel and will all be male Jews. Literally, young virgin men.[57]

Several years ago, I met with a woman who was in her late 70's who claimed she was one of the 144,000. When I confronted her with all of these facts, she looked at me with a blank stare. I pointed out that she was obviously a woman, and that she had been spiritually defiled by having children. Plus she had been a Roman Catholic, not a Jew. She met none of the Bible's requirements to be one of the 144,000. She had no answer.

---

55 *Strong's Exhaustive Concordance*, 2001 (Italics added)
56 Revelation 14:4a (King James Version)
57 *Strong's Exhaustive Concordance*, 2001 (Italics added)

Summary

• The biblical 144,000 are gathered and sealed during the Tribulation, not in the church age, from 33 AD to the end times. Their sealing is secure and permanent.

• The biblical 144,000 are made up of 12,000 male virgins from each of the 12 tribes of Israel.

• Thus the Watchtower's 144,000 are not the biblical 144,000.

JOSEPH FRANKLIN RUTHERFORD'S PROPHETIC ERRORS

Joseph Franklin Rutherford, second president of the Watchtower Society, is alone responsible for the teaching of the 144,000 as the *faithful and discreet slave.*

This teaching, delivered in Washington D.C. in 1935, is still held to be truth by millions of today's members of the Watchtower Society.[58]

Can this teaching by Rutherford be trusted since he made several serious prophetic errors during his presidency of the Watchtower? If he erred in prophecy, what is the guarantee he was right about the 144,000? What does his track record show?

In 1920, Rutherford authored a book titled, *Millions Now Living Will Never Die.* In his book, he declared:

> ...and since the scriptures *definitely fix* the fact that there will be a resurrection of Abraham, Isaac and Jacob and other faithful ones of old, and that these will have the first favor, *we may expect 1925 to witness the return of these faith-*

---

58 *The Watchtower*, February 1, 1999, p. 17

ful men of Israel from the condition of death,
being resurrected and fully restored to perfect
humanity and made the visible, legal represen-
tatives of the new order of things on earth.[59]

Well, 1925 passed and there were no resurrections.

After the failed 1925 prophecy, Rutherford still insisted
on the physical return of these *Ancient Worthies* as he called
them. In 1928, he authored another book called, *Government*
in which he stated that Abraham, Isaac and Jacob, would be
back on earth within a relatively short time.[60]

The 1942 Watchtower publication, *The New World,* states
that in 1930 a house called *Beth-Sarim* (House of Princes)
was built in San Diego, California and was held in trust for
occupancy by Abraham, Isaac and Jacob upon their return.[61]

But the 1975 Yearbook claimed that *Beth-Sarim* was
built in 1929 for the ailing J.F. Rutherford. He reportedly
had a lung condition and was urged to stay in California
because of its exceptionally good climate.[62]

The 1975 Yearbook made no mention of *Beth-Sarim*
being held in trust for the princes' return. It cited Rutherford's *Salvation* book and took a quote out of context to
avoid what had been written earlier.[63]

Abraham, Isaac and Jacob were never resurrected to
become princes on earth,[64] nor did they live at *Beth-Sarim.*

---

59 *Millions Now Living Will Never Die*, 1920, p. 88 (Italics added)
60 *Government*, 1928, p. 276
61 *The New World*, 1942, p. 104, 105
62 *1975 Yearbook of Jehovah' Witnesses*, 1974, p. 194
63 Ibid.
64 Ibid., p. 146

Rutherford died on January 8, 1942. Quietly, *Beth-Sarim* was sold in the late 1940's.

So was *Beth-Sarim* built in 1929 or 1930... and for whom? One of Jehovah's Witnesses at that time said 1925 was a sad year and the hopes of many Witnesses were dashed.

Because of the failed 1925 prophecy, the Watchtower said:

> This view was adjusted in 1950, when further study of the Scriptures indicated that those earthly forefathers of Jesus Christ would be resurrected after Armageddon. See "The Watchtower," November 1, 1950, pages 414-17.[65]

In other words, Rutherford was wrong according to the Watchtower's own words; and he was part of the anointed 144,000. After the failure of his prophecy, Rutherford made an interesting comment:

> When events failed to support his [Rutherford's] expectations, *he humbly told the Brooklyn Bethel family that he had made a fool of himself.*[66]

Rutherford's Books

In Rutherford's *Millions* book, he promoted and sold his book *The Finished Mystery*. Remember, *The Finished Mystery* declared Russell to be the *faithful and wise servant*. If the 144,000 was fulfilled between 33 A.D. and 1935 and they were that *faithful and wise servant*, why was Rutherford promoting and selling *The Finished Mystery* which declared Russell alone to be that servant?

---

65 *Jehovah's Witnesses, Proclaimers of God's Kingdom*, 1993, p. 76
66 *The Watchtower*, December 1, 1993, p. 18 (Italics added)

In 1921, five years after Russell's death, Rutherford authored another book titled, *The Harp of God*, which declared Russell to be that *wise and faithful servant*. There was no mention of the anointed 144,000 as *the faithful and wise servant*. It was still believed to be Russell. Rutherford wrote:

> *Without a doubt, Pastor Russell filled the office* for which the Lord provided and about which he spoke, *and was therefore that wise and faithful servant*, ministering to the household of faith meat in due season.[67]

In his book, *The Harp of God*, Rutherford also promoted Russell's seven books, *Studies In The Scriptures*, including volume seven, *The Finished Mystery*, which stated that Russell was that *faithful and wise servant*.

Then, ten years after Russell's death, Rutherford wrote another book titled, *Deliverance*. In the back pages, he promoted and sold Russell's books, including *The Finished Mystery*.[68]

From the 1920's through the early 1940's, Rutherford wrote a series of twenty books known today as the *rainbow collection*. In the back pages of some of those books, Rutherford promoted *The Harp of God*, which declared Russell to be that *wise and faithful servant*.

By 1931, the *faithful and discreet slave* was identified as the 144,000. However, from 1931 until 1940, Rutherford was *still* promoting his book, *The Harp of God*, identifying Russell as "that servant." In other words, he was promoting

---

67 *The Harp of God*, 1921, p. 239 (Italics added)
68 See *Deliverance*, 1926

two classes of the *faithful and wise servant* at the same time —one as a class of people and one as an individual.

The following "rainbow" titles promoted and sold *The Harp of God*: *Deliverance* (1926), *Creation* (1927), *Government* (1928), *Life* (1929), *Prophecy* (1929), *Light I, II* (1930), *Vindication I* (1931), *Preparation* (1933), *Riches* (1936), *Enemies* (1937), *Salvation* (1939), *Religion* (1940).

In 1962, twenty years after Rutherford's death, the Watchtower was still selling Russell's *Studies In The Scriptures*.[69] They recognized that Rutherford made errors and said:

> Things published were not perfect in the days of Charles Taze Russell, first president of the Watch Tower Bible and Tract Society; nor were they perfect in the days of J. F. Rutherford, the succeeding president. The increasing light on God's Word as well as the facts of history have *repeatedly required that adjustments of one kind or another be made down to the very present time.*[70]

Isn't it lying to change documented historical events and statements? With respect to lying, the *Watchtower* published an article titled, *Honesty and Truthfulness*, which said:

> So lying and other forms of dishonesty are products of Satan, and liars are really showing themselves to be "sons of disobedience."[71]

> A LIE is a false statement made by one to another who is entitled to hear and know the

---

69 Watchtower Cost List, February 1, 1962
70 *The Watchtower*, March 1, 1979, p. 23-24 (Italics added)
71 *The Watchtower*, February 1, 1963, p. 80

truth and which false statement tends toward injury to the other.[72]

Since Rutherford was wrong on so many important points, why would today's companions trust that he was right about the doctrine of the 144,000?

Summary:

• Rutherford alone is responsible for the Watchtower's present-day teaching of the 144,000.

• Rutherford prophesied that Abraham, Isaac and Jacob would return in 1925. It didn't happen.

• A home in San Diego was purchased for the return of Abraham, Isaac and Jacob. The Watchtower later said it was purchased for Rutherford.

• In Rutherford's *Rainbow series* books, he promoted Russell as *the faithful and wise servant.*

• Rutherford believed his 144,000 Jehovah's Witnesses filled the office as the *faithful and wise servant* but still sold Russell's books which taught that Russell alone filled that office.

• Since Rutherford was wrong about the return of Abraham, Isaac and Jacob, how could he be trusted with his teaching of the 144,000?

• How could Rutherford's teaching of the 144,000 be trusted since he promoted the *faithful and wise servant* both as a class and an individual at the same time?

---

72 *The Watchtower,* October 1, 1954, p. 585

A MAJOR CHANGE

The Watchtower knows full well the trap it set for itself. Teaching that the 144,000 was fulfilled in 1935 is no longer working. And others are starting to notice the deception in adding new numbers to the annual Yearbook figures.

In the May 1, 2007 *Watchtower* magazine, a lame attempt was made to wiggle out of the 72-year-old doctrine:

> … "as time has gone by, some Christians baptized after 1935 have had witness borne to them that they have the heavenly hope. (Romans 8:16, 17) Thus it appears that we cannot set a specific date for when the calling of Christians to the heavenly hope ends."[73]

The article seems to suggest that these are replacements for those who have fallen away. Yet it creates a back door excuse to adjust the remnant figure that would have decreased to zero as the original 144,000 sealed in 1935 died off. This way, the continued survival of the Watchtower organization could be secured to maintain spiritual control over the *companions*.

---

73 *The Watchtower,* May 1, 2007, pp. 31

Since 1935, the Watchtower Society has taught its followers that the heavens were closed to any others outside of their 144,000 Jehovah's Witnesses. Now this obscure passage in the May 1, 2007 *Watchtower* effectively cancels, in one moment, this doctrine and blurs the line between the "anointed remnant" and the other *companions.*

It remains to be seen what new standards will be set in place for any of the *companions* who claim to be one of Jehovah's anointed Witnesses. Keep in mind that before this major change, only those Witnesses who came into the organization by 1935 were allowed to take communion because only they had a heavenly hope. And who of these new members of the "anointed remnant" will be allowed into the leadership positions who teach and write official Watchtower material?

Because the Watchtower cannot now set a specific date, as it did for the last 72 years, this *opens the door to an indefinite date.* No one knows when the number of 144,000 will *ever* be fulfilled. If these are "replacements," does this indicate that there are Jehovah's Witnesses who are still falling away? Apparently so.

Throughout their history, there have been major doctrinal shifts which the Watchtower attributes to "advancing in the light of truth." This is another case where new understanding is "received" when time exposes a false teaching or false prophetic date. When the Watchtower has made such bold statements and then changed them, it condemns itself:

> True, there have been those in time past who predicted an "end to the world," even announc-

ing a specific date. Yet, nothing happened. The "end" did not come. They were guilty of false prophesying. Missing was the full measure of evidence required in fulfillment of Bible prophecy. Missing from such people were God's truths and the evidence that he was guiding and using them.[74]

Finally, the Watchtower addressed the changing of major teachings by stating the following:

> It is a serious matter to represent God and Christ in one way, then find that our understanding of the major teachings and fundamental doctrines of the Scriptures was in error, and then after that, to go back to the very doctrines that, by years of study, we had thoroughly determined to be in error. Christians cannot be vacillating —wishy-washy— about such fundamental teachings. What confidence can one put in the sincerity or judgment of such persons?[75]

Earlier, they admitted that things were not perfect in the days of Russell and Rutherford. Now, they are having to admit that they were wrong about the completion of the 144,000. The fact is that the Watchtower Bible and Tract Society will forever need to adjust dates and teachings.

They will attribute it to "advancing in the light of truth." But if the prophecy was false in the first place, any truth that

---

74 *Awake!*, October 8, 1968, p. 23
75 *The Watchtower*, May 15, 1976, p. 298 (Italics added)

comes along will not be an "advance" but will be an embarrassing contradiction. Their leaders know they can never admit to being inspired as the Bible is inspired.[76]

A major change like the 1935 date reveals again the Watchtower for what it really is: a false prophet not inspired by God. Time will forever be the enemy of such false prophets.

When witnessing to a supposedly "Jehovah's Witness," this is their fatal weakness. The Watchtower is not and does not claim to be inspired by God. So we ask why it is necessary to have the "uninspired" Watchtower interpret the "inspired" Bible for you? Why not just read the Bible for yourself?

---

76 II Timothy 3:16 (See *Winning The Witnesses*, Chick Publications)

YOUR WITNESSING STRATEGY

Those who come to your door and claim to be "one of Jehovah's Witnesses" are convinced that's who they are. The majority of Christians also believe that's who they are. However, now you know otherwise.

For over 70 years, they have taught that the only *true* Jehovah's Witnesses are those who came to the Watchtower organization by 1935. Of roughly seven million "Witnesses" worldwide, only a handful of these original Witnesses remain alive today. *Why is this so important?* Several reasons:

• Members of the *faithful and discreet slave* class are the leaders responsible for Watchtower teaching through its publications.

• Without this *faithful and discreet slave* class, the Watchtower Society would eventually crumble, leaving about seven million *other sheep* with no guidance or spiritual direction. These individuals depend on the Watchtower's publications to tell them how to live. They are *forbidden* to read the Bible without the aid of these publications.

Throughout the years, I have interviewed countless "Witnesses." Many have told me with excitement and anticipation that they could not *wait* for the next issue of *The Watchtower* to see what Jehovah had to say to them. On the average, they will read approximately 1,000 pages of Watchtower publications to one page of the Bible.

Now you see the value these dear people place on the Society's publications. Therefore, it is imperative that the 144,000 *faithful and discrete slave* class remain alive to continue satisfying the voracious appetite of its followers… and to maintain control.

This dependency on the Watchtower's publications is the unseen barrier Christians face in their witness to those who claim to be one of Jehovah's Witnesses. It is also their greatest weakness, which soul winners can use to lead them out of bondage to the Watchtower Society.[77]

Getting Started

You need to understand two things before you witness:

• His dependency on the Watchtower.

• His sole view of life is through the lenses of Watchtower interpretation.

Therefore, *it is useless* to argue Bible passages to make your points. Before the individual can come to know Christ, he must first reject the authority of the Watchtower over his mind and life.

You will need to begin with a series of thought-provoking questions designed to undermine Watchtower authority. See

---

77 For more information, see *Winning The Witnesses*, Chick Publications

yourself as one who is planting seeds of doubt in his mind. Regardless of the response, remember the principle of God's creation in the seed: all seeds are designed to sprout and grow.

This principle is true even in weeds. When he first heard the Watchtower message, it was like bad seed planted in his heart. Those "weed seeds" grew and matured and he is now in a cult that he believes represents the very voice of God.

Warning: *do not allow yourself to be sidetracked by letting him change the subject.* Once you do, you might lose an effective witness. You must stay on one subject —and that subject will be the identity of the *faithful and discreet slave.*

Before you begin your witness, you should:

• Pray for the individual. Ask the Lord to lead and guide you with His wisdom.

• Read this book as many times as you can. This way, you will be better prepared and the Holy Spirit will bring key points to your memory.

• Take notes on what you've learned from the summaries of each chapter. Write down the Watchtower publication next to each point. This way, your points will be supported by official Watchtower publications.

• Role play with someone those points you have learned.

• Practice your witnessing strategy. For years, I've gone out publicly looking for Witnesses to speak to. Doing this will give you valuable experience.

• **Do not give this book to them or show it to them**. The Watchtower Society has conditioned its followers to believe that books such as this will contaminate their thinking. This type of control shields their followers from any outside "influence."

The Presentation

Once the "Witnesses" come to your door, please *do not* start any witnessing until you have agreed on a time to meet in the future. They are on a strict schedule in their door-to-door work and will not have time for lengthy conversation.

If they offer you Watchtower literature, take it. They will view this as a potential interest on your part. This will be the time to make your appointment with them.

When they return for the appointment, start with small talk for a few moments. Ask them how long they can stay. This way, you can begin a strategy of which things you will want to bring to their attention.

Ask them how long they've been Jehovah's Witnesses. (This will later prove to be key.)

Do not use your Bible. Your witnessing strategy is to avoid using the Bible *at this time*. Only use the Bible once he decides to exit the Watchtower and is ready for you to witness Christ to him.

After your presentation, he will eventually come to understand two points after he leaves your home:

1. He is *not* a Jehovah's Witness; and…

2. He will finally know that those who make up the real Jehovah's Witnesses came from a fictitious doctrine. This means his message has no substance or merit; it was all made up.

POINT 1: What is a Jehovah's Witness?

Say:

I am not a member of your faith nor have I *ever* been; and I know you are here to bring me to your faith. Because so much is at stake, any reasonable person would ask questions before he would commit his life to another faith. I'm sure you also had questions of those who first introduced you to your faith. Would you give me the same liberty?

Ask:

• *What* is a Jehovah's Witness?

You will be told that they are a worldwide group of people who declare the name of Jehovah.

• But *who* is a Jehovah's Witness?

• Do you believe *you* are a Jehovah's Witness and why?

You may be told that he is of this faith because of the things he does not believe in, like Christmas, Birthdays, Mother's Day, Father's Day, etc.

• But do you believe that your religion is the only one which boldly proclaims the name of God, Jehovah?

Ask:

• You have told me what you believe and don't believe, but what I want to know now is **who** is a Jehovah's Witness?

Chances are they've never been asked this before.

Ask:

• How did you earn the title, Jehovah's Witness?

• How does it apply to you?

• Have you ever researched the history of the title Jehovah's Witnesses?

The "Witness" may refer you to Isaiah 43:10 from their *New World Translation* Bible: "You are my witnesses is the utterance of Jehovah."

Ask:

Have you ever researched *the history* of that title of those who claim to have that name?

Say:

I have done some research and am *very* interested in your opinion. Because you are a member of this faith, I know you would have far better understanding and insight than I would.

Therefore, it is my understanding that the name Jehovah's Witness only applies to the members of the 144,000 as the *faithful and discreet slave.*

I also understand that the number of 144,000 was completed in 1935. If this is true, how can you can claim the name Jehovah's Witness if you came to the organization in the year _____? (Remember when you asked how long they've been in the Watchtower organization?)

You may continue by saying:

If you are one of Jehovah's Witness, are you allowed to write contributing articles to the *Watchtower* and other Watchtower publications?

Why not?

If only the *faithful and discreet slave* receive directions from God to write, then why are you not able to contribute as a collective body to Biblical understanding?

If you cannot contribute to the *Watchtower*, then you can't be one of Jehovah's Witnesses because they are the only ones who receive direction about what to write. Isn't that true?

The Watchtower teaches that in 1931 the *remnant of the 144,000* embraced the name Jehovah's Witnesses.[78]

The Watchtower also teaches that the *great multitude* of Revelation Chapter 7 is a class with an earthly hope.[79]

Would you agree with the Watchtower that you are not a Jehovah's Witness? Isn't that what they teach? Are you allowed to disagree with the Watchtower?

POINT 2: Who is a Jehovah's Witness?

Since you are not a Jehovah's Witness but part of the *great crowd*, who are the real Jehovah's Witnesses?

My research has revealed that the founder of your faith never once taught any doctrine of 144,000 as the *faithful and discreet slave*. He not only claimed to be "that servant," but this teaching about the 144,000 did not come to be until 1935. I don't think your founder was alive in 1935, was he?

At this point, the "Witness" may object and say that what you are now saying is "old light." You may want to say that this is not old light; this is a matter of documented historical record out of the Watchtower's own publications.

Please allow me to finish.

Is it true that only Jehovah's Witnesses (the 144,000) are allowed to partake of Communion?

Is it true that only Jehovah's Witnesses (the 144,000) have the hope of going to heaven?

---

78 Have him write *The Watchtower*, February 15, 1966, p. 119
79 Have him write *The Watchtower*, August 15, 2001, p. 25 (Italics added)

If you still believe you are a Jehovah's Witness, then why can't you take communion or go to heaven? Isn't it because you are part of the *great crowd*, and not a Jehovah's Witness?

If you are unable to fulfill these two requirements, then you can't be a Jehovah's Witness.

My research has also shown that your founder was believed by his followers to be "that servant." But then he died.

A man by the name of Rutherford also believed that your founder filled that office but changed it in 1935. Then he did something unusual: even after the change of the doctrine, he kept selling your founder's books which proclaimed him to be "that servant."

Even in Rutherford's books, he taught that your founder was that faithful servant; then continued to sell those books for five years after he taught that the servant was the 144,000.

Also, Rutherford said that Abraham, Isaac and Jacob were going to return in 1925. Three years after that failed prophecy, he wrote a book that still said those three Old Testament figures were going to return. Rutherford even wrote of a house in San Diego which was built for them to live in when they returned.

Years later the Watchtower claimed home in San Diego was built for Rutherford but never mentioned the true history.

The point of all these issues is that Rutherford *was wrong.* If he was wrong on all these issues, what is your guarantee that he is right with the doctrine of the 144,000?

If he was wrong about the 144,000 being the *faithful and discreet slave* as God's spokesperson, from whom do you get your message as a member of the *great crowd*?

Did you know that the Watchtower admitted that things published in the days of your founder and Rutherford weren't perfect? If this is so, how can you trust Rutherford's interpretation of the 144,000?[80]

If you *really* value truth, what would it be worth to you to research this information, seeing it was published by the *faithful and discreet slave*? If you don't research this, would it be because you are afraid, or even doubt their writings?

This may seem to be a long list of issues to discuss; however, please keep in mind that you are working at compromising the authority of the Watchtower which is holding his mind hostage. Your goal is to eventually lead him to Christ so he can have the real promise of going to heaven.

Remember: **Do not discuss Bible passages**. His interpretation of scripture is what the Watchtower has taught him. If you engage the "Witness" in a Bible discussion, you will be engaging the symptom *not the cause* of how he arrived at his conclusions.

Keep in mind that you are planting seeds, which take time to grow and mature. You may never know what he will do with this information; but I assure you, with time those seeds will grow.

---

80 The *Watchtower*, March 1, 1979, p. 23-24)

WHO EXACTLY *IS* GOING TO HEAVEN?

Since the Watchtower's teaching about the 144,000 has no historical or biblical basis, they are maneuvering to cover the false teaching by hosting a *two-class religion* —a heavenly hope for the supposed 144,000 —and an earthly hope for the *great crowd companions*.

The 144,000 have total authority and control over the *great crowd*. Total adherence and obedience is required by the *great crowd* to the "faithful and discrete slave" class.

According to the Bible, there is no class distinction in the Lord's church. It is made up of *one* body, not two. Cults such as this usually develop a ruling class that demands blind obedience from the follower class.

As the seeds of doubt grow, your witness will eventually need to turn to the Bible. It is one thing to undermine the trust in the Watchtower Society, but that is only half the job.

Once that trust is destroyed, confidence in the Bible must be restored. The following verses will assist you at this stage. For more detailed help, see *Winning the Witnesses*, by this author, published by Chick Publications.

The Bible does not reserve the assurance of Heaven for a select few, but *for all* who trust and believe the message of the gospel of Christ. Jesus promised:

> For God so loved the world, that he gave his only begotten Son, that *whosoever believeth in him should not perish*, but have everlasting life.[81]

The word *whosoever* eliminates any lines of distinction between people. By saying whosoever, Jesus gave His promise of everlasting life to *all* who believe in Him.

In Paul's Epistle to the Romans, he said:

> That if thou shalt confess with thy mouth the Lord Jesus, and shalt believe in thine heart that God hath raised him from the dead, thou shalt be saved. For with the heart man believeth unto righteousness; and with the mouth confession is made unto salvation... For there is no difference between the Jew and the Greek: for the same Lord over all is rich unto all that call upon him. For whosoever shall call upon the name of the Lord shall be saved.[82]

Again, Paul said:

> So we, being many, *are one body in Christ*, and every one members one of another.[83]

> There is *one body*, and one Spirit, even as ye are called in *one hope of your calling*.[84]

---

81 John 3:16 KJV (Italics added)
82 Romans 10:9–10, 12-13 KJV
83 Romans 12:5 KJV (Emphasis added)
84 Ephesians 4:4 KJV (Emphasis added)

For this *one body* Jesus provided *one sacrifice*.

> But this man, after he had offered *one sacrifice* for sins forever, *sat down on the right hand of God*.[85]

Where is Jesus now?

> So then after the Lord had spoken unto them, he was received up into heaven, and sat on the right hand of God.[86]

Jesus tells us the eternal destination for those *whosoevers*?

> In my Father's house are many mansions: if it were not so, I would have told you. *I go to prepare a place for you*. And if I go and prepare a place for you, I will come again, and receive you unto myself; *that where I am, there ye may be also*.[87]

Where Jesus is, those who put their trust and faith in Him will be, also.

In John's first Epistle, he wrote:

> WHOSOEVER believeth that Jesus is the Christ is born of God. For *whatsoever is born of God overcometh the world*: and this is the victory that overcometh the world, even our faith. *Who is he that overcometh the world, but he that believeth that Jesus is the Son of God*.[88]
>
> To *him that overcometh will I grant to sit with*

---

85 Hebrews 10:12 KJV (Emphasis added)
86 Mark 16:19 KJV (Italics added)
87 John 14:1–3 KJV (Italics added)
88 I John 5:1a, 4a–5 KJV (Italics added)

> *me in my throne*, even as I overcame, and am
> set down with my Father in his throne.[89]

Salvation is found only in accepting the work of Jesus'
sacrifice, not in any religious organization.

> Being *justified freely by his grace* through the
> redemption that is in Christ Jesus...[90]
>
> Even the righteousness of God which is by faith
> of Jesus Christ *unto all* and upon all them that
> believe: for there is no difference.[91]

Heaven has never been closed at any time, *especially*
since 1935. It remains open for anyone who confesses Jesus
as Lord and Savior. Even now, Jesus stands waiting at the
door of countless hearts —knocking—and waiting to see
who will hear His voice; waiting to see who will open that
door so He can enter.

> Behold, I stand at the door, and knock: if any
> man hear my voice, and open the door, I will
> come in to him, and will sup with him, and
> he with me.[92]

---

89 Revelation 3:21 KJV (Italics added)
90 Romans 3:24 KJV (Italics added)
91 Romans 3:22 KJV (Italics added)
92 Revelation 3:20 KJV